SELF-DEFENSE...

MENTAL, PHYSICAL and SPIRITUAL BATTLE

By Victoria Grace

Ephesians 6:10-11

The Whole Armor of God

10 Finally, my brethren, be strong in the Lord and in the power of His might. 11 Put on the whole armor of God, that you may be able to stand against the wiles of the devil.

ACKNOWLEDGMENTS

I want to acknowledge my wonderful husband Joseph Saladino who is a constant encouragement to me and has provided Self-defense information and guidance.

My sincerest thanks to God my Lord Jesus Christ.

About the Author

I like spending my time outdoors as I enjoy nature and Photography is my hobby. My writing derives from my everyday life experiences and is inspired by reading the words of God (Bible) every day.

Through Jesus Christ who gives me strength, I can face the reality of my past, lay everything down at the feet of Jesus. To forgive myself as the Lord has forgiven me.

Through all my life's experiences God is always there with me, loving me as it says in Jeremiah 29:11 "For I know the plans I have for you," declares the Lord, "plans to prosper you and not to harm you, plans to give you hope and a future."

(Victoria Grace is pen name used by Gina Saladino a wife and a mother of two daughters.)

Embrace the Power Within You

1 John 4:4 You, dear children, are from God and have overcome them, because the one who is in you is greater than the one who is in the world.

This profound encouragement: The Holy Spirit dwells within you is greater than the spirit who is in the world. It empowers you to face challenges with confidence, knowing that God's indwelling presence provides strength that surpasses any adversary you face.

CONTENTS

PHYSICALLY

God never promises that believers will be immune to suffering. What He does promise is that He will be there to walk through the trials with us. He promises to be beside us when we "pass through the waters" and "walk through the fire" (Isaiah 43:2). He also assures us that He will be there when we "walk through the valley of the shadow of death" (Psalm 23:4). Our life and experiences are lessons and examples for us and for others to learn from. Every day is a new day—a new opportunity to learn something and to discover who we are in God's eyes.

Nowhere is it written that you can't protect yourself or your family. What you should never do is seek revenge or deliberately provoke a confrontation. You must be slow to anger and handle all situations with wisdom. Avoiding confrontation at all costs should always be kept in mind. Fight only to defend yourself and your loved ones and to protect those who can't defend themselves—as a last resort. Train yourself for battle to benefit those under your protection, including yourself. It is perfectly fine to learn self-defense, but remember never to retaliate and always act wisely. If it is possible, as far as it depends on you, live at peace with everyone.

{Luke 11:21: "When a strong man, fully armed, guards his own house, his possessions are undisturbed."}
Be empowered by common sense and the ability to discern your enemies' next move.
Protect your family, others, and yourself.

1. **Avoid confrontation as much as possible.** However, we are also reminded in 2 Timothy 1:7: "For God has not given us a spirit of fear and timidity, but of power, love, and self-discipline." When we feel the need to confront something or someone, it is often because we feel a passion stirred within ourselves. If we keep this scripture in mind and close to our hearts, we will be focused in the right direction should trouble arise.

2. **Fight only to defend yourself.** Psalms 144:1: "Blessed be the LORD my strength, which teaches my hands to war, and my fingers to fight." Pray for strength and guidance, and fight only to defend yourself. Don't live your life by dedicating yourself to an inferior purpose that has no lasting value. Live for God's purpose. Only God can make your life worthwhile, purposeful, and meaningful. Fighting often results in injury, great liability, or worse, so it should always be a last resort.

3. **Fight for the vulnerable.** Psalm 82:3-4: "Give justice to the weak and the fatherless; maintain the right of the afflicted and the destitute. Rescue the weak and the needy; deliver them from the hand of the wicked." Stand up for all that belongs to you and protect those who are preyed upon. Rescue the captives condemned to death and spare those staggering toward their demise. Fighting doesn't always mean physical confrontation—only in cases where danger to yourself or others cannot be avoided through other means.

4. **Defend your loved ones.** John 15:13: "Greater love has

no one than this: to lay down one's life for one's friends." A threat to you is different from someone merely offending or irritating you. If someone punches you in the face, use biblical discernment—even if you know you can retaliate. It's different if someone relentlessly attacks you or tries to harm your loved ones. You must protect yourself and your family using the minimal force necessary to neutralize the threat. Outsmart your opponent by following these principles.

There are situations where you must defend yourself. If you can run, then run. But if you can't, and someone poses a serious threat, you must do what is necessary to stop or prevent harm to all involved. It is perfectly fine to own firearms or take boxing, karate, or other self-defense classes (if legally allowed—check with your local laws). However, remember to never retaliate and always act wisely. Defend only as a last resort, after all other means have been exhausted. Sometimes, just because you can do something doesn't mean you should. Use good communication skills to de-escalate threats or anger directed at you.

If possible, bring up a non-threatening topic to redirect the aggressor's anger. For example, if an attacker says, "I'm going to kick your ass," you might try to de-escalate by saying, "Sir or ma'am, can we please not fight? My family member just died, and I am mourning their loss." This could help divert their anger. At the same time, assess alternate escape paths and defensive measures in case they attack.

Quote: "Arms in the hands of citizens may be used at individual discretion for the defense of the country, the overthrow of tyranny, or private self-defense." John Adams

Isaiah 54:17 But in that coming day no weapon turned against you will succeed. You will silence every voice raised up to accuse you. These benefits are enjoyed by the servants of the LORD; their vindication will come from me. I, the LORD, have spoken!

Let's say someone is armed or tries to run at you and attack you—then that is a different story. You must protect yourself, your family, and your loved ones. You won't be guilty if something happens, as long as you are justified. Be sure to obtain a self-defense policy like CCW Safe or a similar service and be prepared to articulate your side of the story if you acted in fear for your life (consult a qualified attorney). Handle every situation with discernment.

The only time you should ever use deadly force is when your life or your family's life is in imminent danger of serious injury or death (check your local laws and jurisdiction). Many people attack or kill out of anger, but we must be wise. These days, some people act foolishly and irresponsibly. Put your full trust in God and use wisdom in all situations. If you love the Lord God with all your heart and soul and love your neighbor as yourself, it changes the way you approach conflicts.

Mark 12:30-31 says:
"Love the Lord your God with all your heart and with all your soul and with all your mind and with all your strength. The second is this: 'Love your neighbor as yourself.' There is no commandment

greater than these."

The Bible also speaks about when and how to act in self-defense. Again, avoid confrontation at all costs. We have a right to defend ourselves but must do so wisely. Anticipate an attack so you can plan your response accordingly. Do what you must to defend yourself, but always act in righteousness.

Isaiah 54:14 says:
"In righteousness you shall be established; You shall be far from oppression."

The best course of action is to remove yourself from danger and call 911 immediately with a full description of the person(s) or vehicle involved. Remember, God says, "Do not repay evil with evil."

Psalms 18:34:
"He trains my hands for battle; He strengthens my arm to draw a bronze bow."

We need protection to survive life's impossible threats and strength to respond to life's challenging circumstances. If there were no troubles or challenges, we wouldn't need to defend ourselves. If there were no life-threatening situations, there would be no need to survive them. God doesn't promise to eliminate our troubles, but He does promise to give us strength to face life's challenges and protection from life-threatening troubles. Eternal life is also promised to those who believe in Him.

John 3:16:
"For God so loved the world that He gave His one and only Son, that whoever believes in Him shall not perish but have eternal life."

Defense (Self-Defense)

Psalm 33:16-19:
"The king is not saved by a mighty army; a warrior is not delivered by great strength. A horse is a false hope for victory; nor does it deliver anyone by its great strength. Behold, the eye of the Lord is on those who fear Him, on those who hope for His lovingkindness."

God calls and guides us when we are faced with challenges. Throughout the Bible, God called His people during difficult situations. We are often reluctant to follow God's commands because they require full commitment. Fear becomes a part of our disobedience. Therefore, we must fully trust God, knowing He is in control of everything, and use His wisdom to avoid altercations. It is imperative that we obey when God calls us to act for His name and glory. To obey His commands, we must have strong faith and believe that God is always with us.

We Need Discernment

Job 34:4:
"Let us discern for ourselves what is right; let us learn together what is good."

Rescue the weak and needy. Help them escape the power of the wicked. Only through discernment can we push back our enemies; only through the power of knowledge and wisdom can we triumph over our foes. Trust in the Lord, not in your weapon. Do not rely on yourself or your weapon for salvation. The Lord will disgrace your enemies when you trust in Him. He will give you victory.

Obey the Law

None of these views advocate rebelling against or refusing to obey the law. Wherever you find yourself threatened, you must remain a responsible citizen.

Matthew 5:9:
"Blessed are the peacemakers, for they will be called children of God."

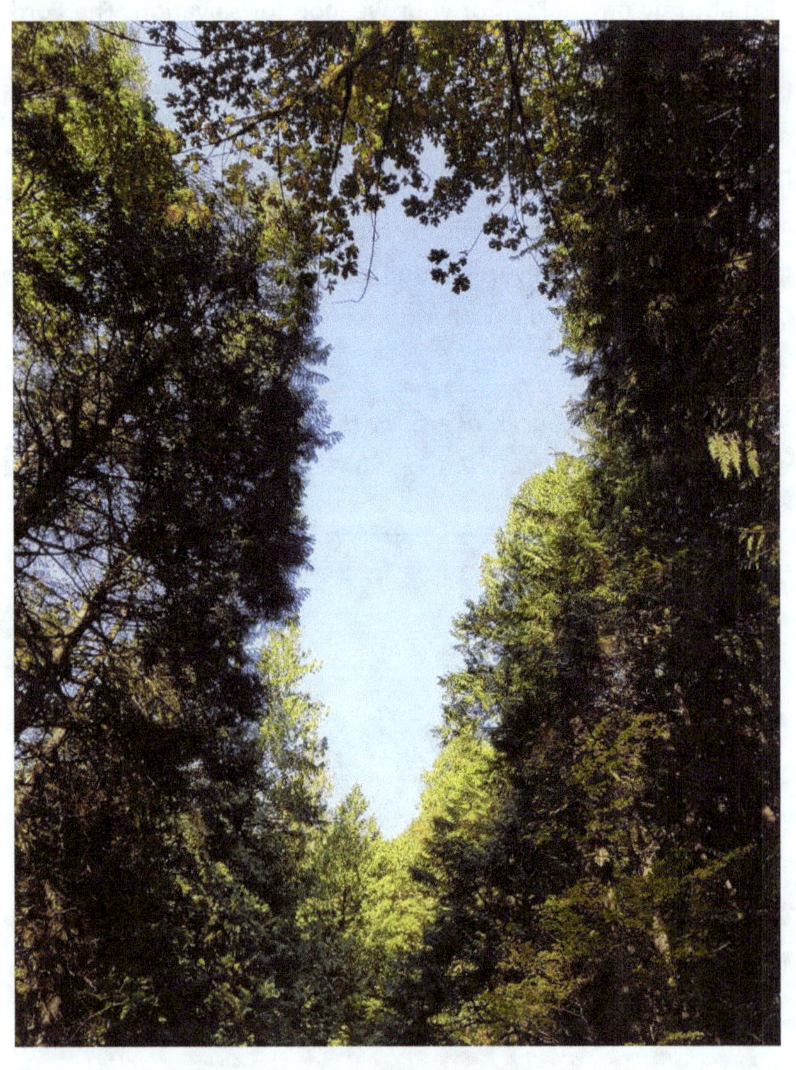

Use force only as a last resort. Study and practice self-defense to avoid causing injury or death.

We live in a world where unfairness and injustice often seem to triumph. When wrong seems right, and darkness relentlessly hovers over you, standing up for what is right becomes a daily battle. Sometimes, giving up feels like the easiest option, and you may feel tempted to succumb to the lure of unrighteousness. Your eyes may become a fountain of tears, and your heart burdened with sadness and sorrow. Yet, through it all, you will discover God's everlasting love. God also comforts you during struggles and distress. Stand firm and trust in the Lord God Almighty.

1 Corinthians 9:26
"Therefore I do not run like someone running aimlessly; I do not fight like a boxer beating the air."

Discipline your body—eat healthily, exercise, take self-defense courses, take vitamins, hydrate regularly, and consult your doctor as needed. Ensure you get the proper amount of sleep. Give careful thought to the paths you take and remain steadfast in all your ways. Guarding yourself means guarding your thoughts, feelings, desires, will, and choices, as these dictate your next move. Your mind reflects who you really are, beyond just your actions or words. God examines your motives, not simply your outward appearance or ulterior intentions.

2 Corinthians 4:18
"We fix our eyes not on what is seen, but on what is unseen, since what is seen is temporary, but what is unseen is eternal."

Your troubles should not diminish your faith. Do not resent your troubles but view them as opportunities to grow. They help keep you humble and focused on eternal things rather than this brief life. After all, God is in control of everything.

Luke 1:17

"That we should be saved from our enemies and from the hands of those who hate us."

In the face of challenges, you may wonder where God is in all of this. God has never left you; He allows things to happen to give you opportunities to do what is right. Sin in the world is a result of fallen humanity, not God's fault. It is the result of humans' wrongful actions. As Christians and followers of Jesus Christ, we must not view our enemies as scary or menacing but instead see them through God's eyes. With strong faith and God's guidance, you can display self-confidence before your enemies. You may miss God's presence and guidance if you are not focused on what is good for you and those you love.

Proverbs 24:16

"For the righteous falls seven times and rises again, but the wicked stumble in times of calamity."

Adversity can be useful. It reveals your true character and helps you grow stronger. The difficulties you face today are preparing you for more challenging situations in the future.

Isaiah 26:3

"You will keep in perfect peace those whose minds are steadfast because they trust in you."

Always do things in the proper order. Even if you fight with all your might, you can still lose if you don't train, practice, and follow the correct sequence of actions (which could result in being sued, arrested, injured, or worse). Do not compromise your standards for doing what is right. Acting rightly earns respect and honor.

Micah 7:8

"Rejoice not over me, O my enemy; when I fall, I shall rise; when I sit in darkness, the Lord will be a light to me."

Use your hands wisely. Understand basic techniques by analyzing and anticipating your enemy's moves.

Deuteronomy 28:7

"The Lord shall cause your enemies who rise against you to be defeated before you; they will come out against you one way and flee before you seven ways."

The Golden Rule often seems forgotten in today's world. People think more about what they can get rather than what they can give. Are you making a positive impact on your children and those around you? To make an impact on someone's life, take the initiative to do good for others. This is the foundation of goodness and mercy—the kind God shows us every day.

Hebrews 5:14

"But solid food is for the mature, for those who have their powers of discernment trained by constant practice to distinguish good from evil."

Train your conscience, senses, mind, and body to distinguish between right and wrong through consistent practice. Can you recognize temptation from your enemies? When you face difficulties, do not be discouraged. No circumstance is too challenging when you trust in the Lord. In your time of need, God is on your side—no enemy is undefeatable. God will provide a way out; you need only trust Him. He will keep you steady and secure.

Proverbs 3:5

"Trust in the Lord with all your heart and lean not on your own understanding."

Psalms 73:25-26

"Whom have I in heaven but You? And besides You, I desire nothing on earth. My flesh and my heart may fail, but God is the strength of my heart and my portion forever."

True victory lies in your perspective, priorities, and source of power. Live to win by saving lives—including your own. Every soul you lead to Jesus Christ as their Savior is the ultimate victory.

Train and condition yourself mentally, physically, and spiritually. Such preparation will help you become a better person and create peace around you.

Romans 8:37

"No, in all these things we are more than conquerors through Him who loved us."

You are chosen to receive the gift of being a warrior and conqueror to rescue and help those who cannot help themselves by leading them to the cross of our Lord Jesus Christ. This is the greatest gift you can give to another person. However, this does not mean you should look for trouble or attack anyone who seems to present a threat to you or those around you. If possible, avoid violence at all costs.

Deuteronomy 1:42

"And the Lord said to me, 'Say to them, "Do not go up nor fight, for I am not among you; otherwise, you will be defeated before your enemies."'"

Pray for guidance from the Lord. There will be times when your enemies seem bigger than you. Sometimes, God must humble you to bring you victory. You may need a new attitude, but you will not change until God humbles you through pain, suffering, humiliation, or defeat.

Are you willing to sacrifice everything and leave it all behind to serve a higher purpose, not for yourself alone but for others? You are here to follow the path set before you and to guide others along it. It is time to show the world the **power of God!** The world can change radically, in a positive and loving way. Communicate your ideas, share your common goals and purpose, and show care and love one person at a time. By doing this, you will create a peaceful, harmonious, and prosperous new world where God's name is glorified. You are God's instruments to bring hope, love, and life to all mankind.

Follow the law and always remember what is right—what truly matters.

John 16:33
"I have told you these things, so that in Me you may have peace. In this world, you will have trouble. But take heart! I have overcome the world."

Joshua 10:19
"Do not stay there yourselves; pursue your enemies and attack them from the rear. Do not allow them to enter their cities, for the Lord your God has delivered them into your hand."

Timing is crucial. When should you fight? If you must fight, it should only be to defend yourself, your loved ones, or those under your protection. Furthermore, fight only as a last resort, to save lives. As someone who has vowed to protect the vulnerable, remember that triumph is part of your strategy.

Do not live life irresponsibly as though it were a never-ending party. Instead, take pleasure in what you do through God and enjoy life as the gift it truly is. True enjoyment in life comes from following God's guidelines for living. You will experience true joy when you take each day as a gift from God, thank Him for it, and serve Him in it.

Psalm 95:1-5

"Come, let us sing for joy to the Lord; let us shout aloud to the Rock of our salvation. Let us come before Him with thanksgiving and extol Him with music and song. For the Lord is the great God, the great King above all gods. In His hand are the depths of the earth, and the mountain peaks belong to Him. The sea is His, for He made it, and His hands formed the dry land."

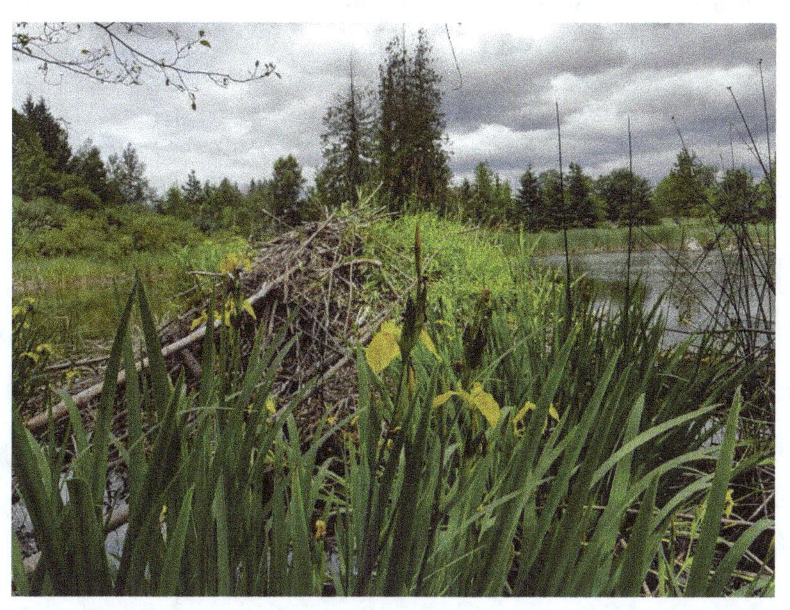

MENTALLY

Seek to be mentally and spiritually strong. Mental strength leads to peace.

Romans 8:6

"If people's thinking is controlled by the sinful self, there is death. But if their thinking is controlled by the Spirit, there is life and peace."

Practicing. Conditioning. Focus

Safety is paramount. Whatever you do, ensure it is done with care and due diligence. Whether you are exercising or training, seek professional guidance to develop an effective plan to maximize your life's victories.

Isaiah 42:5

"Thus says God the Lord, who created the heavens and stretched them out, who spread out the earth and its offspring, who gives breath to the people on it and spirit to those who walk in it:"

You live in an imperfect world; reducing your expectations can help you navigate the inherent unfairness of life. It is difficult to accept that the swiftest and strongest do not always win, the wise remain poor, and the skillful often go unrecognized for their talents. Humanity has twisted life into something God never intended it to be. Keep your perspective by remembering that you live in a fallen world. Society tends to honor wealth, attractiveness, and success over wisdom. It is disheartening to see people strive to look important in man's eyes while damaging their relationship with God.

God commands you to do good to others, especially those who are unfortunate and unloved. Offering sacrificial love to others pleases and glorifies God. **LOVE** is the greatest good you can do for anyone. **LOVE** is sacrificing, whatever it may require, to please God. **LOVE** is the answer to many of life's seemingly indefinable and unexplained circumstances. Love sacrificially, as God loves you, by sacrificing His only begotten Son, Jesus Christ.

1 Corinthians 13:4-8

"Love is patient, love is kind. It does not envy, it does not boast, it is not proud. It does not dishonor others, it is not self-seeking, it is not easily angered, it keeps no record of wrongs. Love does not delight in evil but rejoices with the truth. It always protects, always trusts, always hopes, always perseveres. Love never fails. But where there are prophecies, they will cease; where there are tongues, they will be stilled; where there is knowledge, it will pass away."

Giving thanks reminds you of how much you already have. By giving thanks continually, you gain a deeper appreciation for your blessings. When you focus on what you have instead of what you lack, you will find greater happiness. When you thank God for the things you usually take for granted, your perspective changes. You begin to realize that you could not exist without God's merciful blessings.

Job 33:4

"The Spirit of God has made me, and the breath of the Almighty gives me life."

Find ways to remain constantly obedient to God's leading in your life. True peace comes from knowing that God is in control of everything. Repentance is key to spiritually cleansing your soul and spirit. Recognizing that you are a sinner and seeking forgiveness is essential.

Acts 3:19
"Repent, then, and turn to God, so that your sins may be wiped out, that times of refreshing may come from the Lord."

Job 32:8
"But it is a spirit in man, and the breath of the Almighty gives them understanding."

When you keep your eyes focused on God, you are reminded of His love for you and realize that you truly have nothing to worry about. God has a wonderful plan for your life, and part of that plan includes taking care of you. Even in difficult times, when it feels like God doesn’t care, you can put your trust in Him and focus on His kingdom. God will take care of your every need.

The Devil attacks when you're weak physically and emotionally.

Ephesians 6:11

"Put on the whole armor of God, that you may be able to stand against the wiles of the devil."

In the Christian life, we battle against powerful evil forces headed by Satan, a vicious fighter. To withstand his attacks, we must depend on God's strength and use every piece of His armor. As we battle against the evil rulers of the unseen world, we must fight with the strength that comes from the Holy Spirit.

We need supernatural power to defeat the evil ones. God has provided the Holy Spirit within us and His armor surrounding us. All the power of hell will not prevail.

Ephesians 6:12

"For our struggle is not against flesh and blood, but against the rulers, against the authorities, against the powers of this dark world and against the spiritual forces of evil in the heavenly realms."

The evil rulers, satanic beings, and evil princes of darkness are not human but fallen angels over whom Satan (darkness) has control. They are not mere fantasies; they are very real. We face a powerful army whose goal is to defeat Christ's church (love and light). When we believe in Christ and align ourselves with God's love and light, we become enemies of the darkness. The darkness will use every possible device to sway us away from God (love and light).

Although we are assured of victory, we must engage in the battle until Christ comes because darkness constantly battles against those who are in the light. We need supernatural power to defeat the darkness, and God has provided us with His Holy Spirit within us and His armor surrounding us. We must depend on God's strength and use every piece of the armor to withstand the darkness.

If we feel discouraged, let us remember Jesus' words to Peter in **Matthew 16:16**:
"Upon this rock, I will build my church (love and light), and all the power of darkness shall not prevail against it."

Ephesians 6:13
"Therefore put on the full armor of God, so that when the day of evil comes, you may be able to stand your ground, and after you have done everything, to stand."

Satan fights with lies, and sometimes his lies sound like the truth. Satan attacks your heart—the seat of your emotions, self-worth, and trust. He sends enemies to attack you mentally, physically, and spiritually. These attacks may make you feel worthless and hopeless.

Be sure to put on the full armor of God:

- **The belt of truth** to defeat the lies of the enemy.
- **The breastplate of righteousness** to protect your heart.
- **The shoes of peace** to give you the motivation to continue proclaiming the gospel, even to your enemies.

- **The shield of faith** to protect you from the flaming arrows of the enemy.
- **The helmet of salvation** to guard your mind from doubting God's power.
- **The sword of the Spirit**, the Word of God, as your weapon of offense to protect yourself, others, and your loved ones.
- Lastly, **prayer**—pray continually, even for your enemies.

Each piece of the armor represents essential principles for living a peaceful and victorious life.

By incorporating these practices and maintaining discipline, you will always be ready to face the challenges and temptations of the enemy, fully protected by the armor of God.

Weapons of Warfare

By abiding by these scriptural truths, you actively participate in the spiritual warfare that surrounds you, equipped with the truth of Jesus Christ, ready to confront and overcome the adversary.

Isaiah 54:17

"No weapon forged against you will prevail, and you will refute every tongue that accuses you. This is the heritage of the servants of the Lord, and this is their vindication from me," declares the Lord."

If you are impressed by or afraid of any weapons, armies, or powerful people, remember that God alone can truly rescue you from fear and oppression. You must place your confidence in God because He alone can protect your life. Trust God always in every circumstance, as He is always on your side. Put your full confidence in God, and He will guide you here on earth toward your eternal destination. God is with you always, and no one can harm you.

1 Peter 5:8-9

"Be alert and of sober mind. Your enemy, the devil, prowls around like a roaring lion looking for someone to devour. Resist him, standing firm in the faith, because you know that the family of believers throughout the world is undergoing the same kind of sufferings."

The world isn't always a perfect or safe place to dwell. You may encounter trials and tribulations. In your weaknesses, you may focus on your troubles so much that you forget to watch out for danger. Satan uses your problems to attack you when you are vulnerable. During suffering, trials, and sorrows, seek God. With firm and strong faith in God through Christ Jesus, you can overcome worldly desires and resist the devil's temptations. Be constant in prayer, and in your meditation, acknowledge that God is in control of everything. God always prevails—Christ Jesus is our victory.

Deuteronomy 28:7

"The LORD will grant that the enemies who rise up against you will be defeated before you. They will come at you from one direction but flee from you in seven."

Knowing God means that when trouble comes, you count it as a blessing and turn to Him for help. God allows both good and bad to come into your life to strengthen your faith and help you remain faithful. When you are blessed with prosperity, turn to God and ask Him to help you use your blessings faithfully. After all, He is God, and you are not. Despite everything you do, God calls you His children and loves you regardless of your iniquities and shortcomings.

James 4:7

"Submit yourselves, then, to God. Resist the devil, and he will flee from you."

Although God and Satan are at war, you don't need to wait and see who will win. God has already defeated Satan. When Jesus Christ returns, Satan and all that he stands for will be eliminated forever. Satan is here now; however, he is trying to win people over to his evil cause. With the Holy Spirit in our lives, we can resist Satan, and he will flee from us.

Humble yourself before the Lord, realizing that your worth comes from God alone. God reaches out to you in love and gives you worth and dignity, despite your human shortcomings.

SPIRITUALLY

Divine Protection

God's Protection in the Midst of Danger, Diseases, etc.

God doesn't promise a world free from danger and diseases, but He does promise help whenever we face danger.

Psalms 91

"We live within the shadow of the Almighty, sheltered by the God who is above all gods. This I declare: that he alone is my refuge, my place of safety; he is my God, and I am trusting him. For he rescues you from every trap and protects you from the fatal plague. He will shield you with his wings! They will shelter you. His faithful promises are your armor. Now you don't need to be afraid of the dark anymore, nor fear the dangers of the day; nor dread the plagues of darkness, nor disasters in the morning. Though a thousand fall at your side, though ten thousand are dying around you, the evil will not touch you. I will see how the wicked are punished, but I will not share it. For Jehovah is my refuge! I choose the God above all gods to shelter me. How then can evil overtake me or any plague come near? For he orders his angels to protect you wherever you go. They will steady you with their hands to keep you from stumbling against the rocks on the trail. You can safely meet a lion or step on poisonous snakes; yes, even trample them beneath your feet! For the Lord says,

'Because he loves me, I will rescue him; I will make him great because he trusts in my name. When he calls on me, I will answer; I will be with him in trouble and rescue him and honor him. I will satisfy him with a full life and give him my salvation.'"

In this chapter, you learn that no matter what surrounds you, God's protection is upon you. God is your refuge—a shelter when you are afraid. Your faith in God and our Lord Jesus Christ as **Protector** will carry you through all the dangers and fears of life.

This should be a picture of our trust—trading all your fears for faith in our Lord Jesus Christ, no matter the nature of your fear. It helps you concentrate on using your life for eternal good, not just for fleeting moments of pleasure. It may appear as though you are surrounded by enemies (evil), but the Lord surrounds you with His love and protection.

Victory Through the Lord Jesus Christ: You Are More Than a Conqueror

Your ultimate triumph over mental, physical, and spiritual adversity is secured in Jesus Christ.

Romans 8:37

"No, in all these things we are more than conquerors through him who loved us."

You can be assured that through Jesus Christ's love, you will be victorious. This assurance should empower you to face life's battles and challenges with the confidence that nothing can separate you from God's love and victory through our Lord Jesus Christ. Trust in God's intervention in your battles. Stand firm in your faith, witnessing God's power and grace in achieving victory. By embracing these truths and living them out, you can navigate the complexities of spiritual warfare. Your journey is marked by faith, God's protective care, and ultimate triumph.

Proverbs 11:14

"For lack of guidance a nation falls, but victory is won through many advisers."

To be a wise leader at home, at work, or in church, you need to be open to others' counsel and advice. Do not be blinded by bias, wrong impressions, or emotions. A good leader uses wise counselors, as one person's perspective is limited. If you seek guidance from God, your Creator, you will avoid injustice. Humble yourself and seek guidance from the Lord. After considering all the facts, make your decision wisely.

Fruit of the Spirit

Galatians 5:22-23

22 But the fruit of the Spirit is love, joy, peace, forbearance, kindness, goodness, faithfulness, 23 gentleness and self-control. Against such things there is no law.

(LOVE)
From the Greek word **"Agape"**, this kind of love depicts love by choice. It is a selfless love, asking nothing in return. Many of us struggle with this character trait. Love is so central to Christianity that scripture says without it, you don't know God (**1 John 4:8**). Jesus taught that love of neighbor (and love of God) is the greatest commandment. Once you learn to defend yourself, you can effectively defend others. You may even find yourself in a situation where you're forced to defend or protect complete strangers—or even your enemy.

(JOY)
Joy is much deeper than mere happiness and is rooted in God Himself. Self-defense and self-confidence can bring you joy! You will marvel at the capability of the human body. God created our bodies with far greater abilities than we can imagine! Find joy in the strength God has given you.

(PEACE)
The word "peace" comes from the Greek word **"eirene"**. It expresses the idea of wholeness, completeness, or tranquility in the soul that is unaffected by outward circumstances or pressures. Peace of mind comes when you learn how to handle

yourself under stress. The longer you train, the more you realize that in a fight, you are not forced to be a victim. **You** dictate the circumstances, and knowing that will bring you peace. This is particularly true if you are a victim of bullying or a woman learning self-defense.

(PATIENCE)
Self-defense is not an art of instant gratification—it is quite the opposite. In many martial arts, a person can earn a black belt in four years or less, with frequent belt promotions along the way. In contrast, the average Jiu Jitsu practitioner takes 8 to 12 years to earn their black belt. Those **patients** enough to earn a black belt quickly realize they are just getting started. In the beginning, you will lose, and frustration is common. There is a saying in Jiu Jitsu that I will paraphrase for you: *"In Jiu Jitsu, you either win or you learn—you never lose."*

(KINDNESS)
Kindness is goodness in action, sweetness of disposition, gentleness in dealing with others, benevolence, and affability. The word describes the ability to act for the welfare of those who test your patience. The Holy Spirit removes abrasive qualities from the character of someone under His control, and self-defense training can sharpen you in these qualities as you progress. Some might think martial arts are the last place you'd find kindness, but quite the contrary! The kindness of your training partner, combined with the experience of the instructor, guarantees an environment that is both safe and fun. The kindest thing I can do is help others become better—something that may one day save their life or the life of someone they love.

(GOODNESS)

Goodness most simply means "uprightness of heart and life." Our testimony is on display everywhere. We have the opportunity to display goodness in a biblical way. You want to be like Jesus—not just at church but in all aspects of life. When things aren't going your way, you must display biblical uprightness of heart and life. When God gives you the opportunity to share the Good News, you won't be seen as a hypocrite if you've displayed biblical goodness.

(FAITHFULNESS)

Faithfulness is committing oneself to something or someone. Being faithful requires personal resolve not to wander away from commitments or promises. Jesus said, *"I will never leave you or forsake you."* If, by God's grace, your training and practice bring you closer to faith, then your faithfulness will extend far beyond your practice and into discipleship.

(GENTLENESS)

Biblical gentleness is a disposition that is even-tempered, tranquil, balanced in spirit, unpretentious, and under control. The word is best translated as *"meekness,"* not indicating weakness, but rather maintaining control over your power and strength. A person displaying gentleness pardons transgressions and personal insults, corrects faults, and rules their spirit well. This is the heart of Jiu Jitsu! Jiu Jitsu literally means **"The Gentle Art"**—the perfect martial art for Christians.

(SELF-CONTROL)

The Greek word used in **Galatians 5:23** is **"egkrateia"**, meaning *"strong, having mastery, able to control one's thoughts and* *actions."* You will realize that you're not as tough as you thought, and self-control is key to dealing with the many frustrations of life.

FRUIT OF THE SPIRIT

The Christian should display the Fruit of the Spirit in all areas of life. Basic Jiu Jitsu training can help increase your spiritual fruit. Ignore the voice in your head telling you that you're too old, too fat, or too inflexible to try Jiu Jitsu. Your body is capable of far more than you give it credit for!

Living Out Your Victory

Here is the proofread version of your text with corrections for grammar, punctuation, and clarity while retaining the original meaning:

Your actions and decisions can be influenced by victory through Jesus Christ. Live out your faith courageously, making choices and decisions that reflect your trust in God's supremacy over any evil forces.

Proverbs 29:5
"Those who flatter their neighbors are spreading nets for their feet."

You want to be liked, so you are vulnerable to flattery—a dangerous trap. To avoid falling into it, be realistic about yourself. Know when you deserve praise and when you need to be rebuked. Knowledge and wisdom can make you immune to flattery and protect you from being manipulated by people. Know who you are in God and be confident in yourself.

Isaiah 40:31
"But they that wait upon the LORD shall renew their strength; they shall mount up with wings as eagles; they shall run, and not be weary; and they shall walk, and not faint."

Life's challenges often beset you relentlessly. The dark tunnel may seem endless, and you may struggle to see where you are headed. Unexpected events can occur in the blink of an eye—circumstances that can alter your life and bring you to your knees in despair. Perhaps this is God's way of showing you to humble yourself—to pray and beg for His grace and mercy.

You need to stop worrying, stop being distracted by the world, and listen to the Lord. Stop, drop everything, and keep your focus on Christ Jesus. Often, you forget what really matters in your life. God should always be your priority. As the Bible says:

Matthew 6:33
"But seek first the kingdom of God and His righteousness, and all these things shall be added to you."

2 Thessalonians 3:3
"But the Lord is faithful, and He will strengthen you and protect you from the evil one."

God's commitment to protect, strengthen, and guard you against the evil one is a promise and a beacon of hope during times of uncertainty and spiritual warfare. His protection is both sure and steadfast.

Psalms 2:4
"He that sits in the heavens shall laugh: The Lord shall have them in derision."

Nothing is guaranteed in life. Your ability to find humor and laughter in any given situation is a gift to yourself. Let's face it—life is full of quirks and contradictions. To gain new perspectives and unlock your key to happiness, embrace a sense of humor. Look for humor in everything, in every circumstance, and in every situation. Laugh more and live a happy life.

Through Christ, we have gained access by faith into this grace in which we stand, and we rejoice in the hope of the glory of God. To exercise authority over our enemy, you must remain connected to the Lord Jesus Christ—your source of power. This involves daily submission to God's Word and daily prayer.

SUMMARY

It is great to be alive and dwell in the presence of our Lord and Savior Jesus Christ. We are put on earth to love and share God's love with all. Our lives and our experiences are lessons and examples for us and for others to learn from. Every day is a new day—a new opportunity to learn something and to discover who we are in God's eyes.

I pray we live each day to please God alone. May all our troubles and woes turn into blessings that glorify our Lord and Savior Jesus Christ. May our thoughts, the words we speak, and our actions be pleasing to God. Live life as if today is our last day on earth, but plan as if we are to live forever. May God's will be done through us.

It is easy for the righteous to grow discouraged. This calls for the practice of tough faith—the kind of faith that is not dependent on circumstances. It is the kind of faith that perseveres when the going gets tough, sustained by the confident belief that *"all things work together for good for those who love the Lord"* (**Romans 8:28**).

God never promises that believers will be immune to suffering. What He does promise is that He will be there to walk through the trials with us. He promises to be beside us when we *"pass through the waters"* and *"walk through the fire"* (**Isaiah 43:2**). He also assures us that He will be there when we *"walk through the valley of the shadow of death"* (**Psalm 23:4**).

What is the quality of your faith? When life turns sour, do you turn to God, or do you question Him—or even curse Him? One of the keys to perseverance is learning the promises of God's Word (such as **Philippians 4:6-7, 11-13, and 19**) and claiming them in prayer when faced with the challenges of life.

A Simple Sinner's Prayer

("For all have sinned and fall short of the glory of God." — Romans 3:23)

Dear Heavenly Father,

I come to You in the name of Jesus Christ. I acknowledge to You that I am a sinner, and I am sorry for my sins and the life that I have lived; I need Your forgiveness.

I believe that Your only Son, Jesus Christ, shed His precious blood on the cross at Calvary and died for my sins. I am now willing to repent, confess, and turn from my sin. You said in the Bible that if I confess with my mouth and believe in my heart that God raised Jesus Christ from the dead, I shall be saved.

I confess Jesus Christ as my Lord and Savior. With my heart, I believe that God raised Jesus from the dead. At this very moment, I accept Jesus Christ as my own personal Lord and Savior, and according to His Word, right now I am saved. Amen.

www.ingramcontent.com/pod-product-compliance
Lightning Source LLC
Chambersburg PA
CBHW070339120526
44590CB00017B/2950